THINK TWICE

THINK TWICE

An Entertaining Collection of Choices

Bret Nicholaus and Paul Lowrie

Ballantine Books • New York

"I resent the limitations of my own imagination."
WALT DISNEY

"Thank you" to the following people:

Family and close friends, for believing so strongly in these books ever since that "hot-air balloon" took off.

Everyone at Grace Church of LaGrange, for your seemingly endless support of all that I do. You mean a lot to me.
—Bret Nicholaus

Josh, my nephew, and Shannon, my niece, who never make me think twice about having fun.
—Paul Lowrie

We would mutually like to thank

Randy Bray, for taking that plane from Denver to Chicago; it's not *every* title that's conceived at 35,000 feet!

Cathy Repetti, associate publisher, and Joseph Durepos, literary agent, for their dedication to this project.

WELCOME

Life and choices, choices and life . . . two words that seem to be infinitely woven together for each and every one of us. Some choices we make are relatively trivial, like whether we wear the black pants or the blue pants, whether we go out for dinner or eat at home, or whether we answer the telephone or let the machine pick it up. Other choices are more difficult, like whether to get married or remain single, whether to support or oppose the death penalty. Easy decisions and hard ones, our lives revolve around them.

The book you are holding, *Think Twice,* puts an amusing new twist on decision-making. Much like our previous *Conversation Piece* books, this title was designed with the word *entertaining* at the forefront. We do not force you into confrontational situations by asking questions about political issues or personal ethics, nor do we bore you with the mundane type of choices you're used to making in your daily life. Our questions and corresponding choices will encourage you to smile, to laugh, to dream about tomorrow, and to recall famous moments from days gone by. There are choices here for everyone: history buffs, sports fans, world travelers, nature lovers, creative thinkers, children—the list goes on. Regardless of who you are or what you enjoy, *Think Twice* will entertain you in a way that no other book can.

And there are so many great opportunities and places for this book to be enjoyed. For example:

- Dinner parties
- Family gatherings
- New groups (icebreaker questions)
- Trips in the car with other people
- Creative brainstorming sessions
- Fun debates with family or friends
- School classrooms
- Writing assignment topics
- Personal reflection

· Anytime you want to learn more about yourself or others

So how do you use the book? It's easy! Read a question and ponder the two choices available. Then, make a decision—A or B. Don't give in to the temptation to say, "I can't decide." Just like in real life, make a decision based on the options that are available to you. Then, *after* you have chosen an answer, the sky's the limit: offer alternative answers, expand the question itself, or come up with new questions and choices of your own. Indeed, every page will stretch the horizon of your thoughts and conversations.

We hope you will thoroughly enjoy *Think Twice* and have as much fun using the book as we've had creating it!

—Bret Nicholaus and Paul Lowrie

THINK TWICE—
THE GAME

Object

To learn interesting facts about other people while trying to accumulate the most points.

What You'll Need

This book, four or more people, paper, and pencils.

Rules

1. Gather a group of people and have them sit in a circle or otherwise conversational seating arrangement.

2. Give each person several sheets of paper and a pen or pencil. On one sheet, each person writes his/her name and below it the names of all other people that will be playing. This is the scoring sheet and should remain with each player throughout the game.

3. Pick one person to be the initial moderator, who will then read any question from the book and its corresponding choices, A and B.

4. Players should be given about sixty seconds to think of their choices. Then, every player, including the moderator, writes his/her "choice" letter (A or B) on a small piece of paper (make certain that each player writes his/her name on the paper as well). The paper is then folded and dropped in a designated container (like a popcorn bowl).

5. At this point, each player silently thinks about who chose A and who chose B. Then, next to each person's name on the name list, each player writes the letter that is *believed* to be the letter that person chose. The moderator should allow about two minutes for players to write their guesses.

6. When all guesses have been written, the moderator begins by telling what his/her choice was. Explaining why you chose that answer makes the game even more fun.

7. After everyone has told his/her actual answer (which the moderator should now verify by looking at the papers in the box), each player counts up how many he/she correctly guessed. The winner for the round is the person with the most correct guesses (each correct guess is worth one point).

NOTE: *Each player, including the moderator, should always count his/her personal choice as a correct answer (one point). Also, be sure to allow each player to have a turn as the moderator.*

8. The player with the most correct guesses at the end of all the rounds is the *Think Twice* champion.

FINAL NOTE: *Players should always write their honest answers; this is not designed to be a bluffing game. Remember that the true purpose of the contest is to encourage fun conversation while learning out-of-the-ordinary information about other people.*

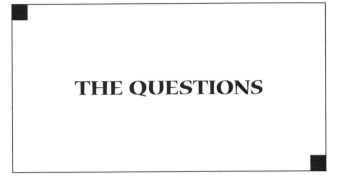

THE QUESTIONS

1 If you had the opportunity to witness either of the following events in person, which one would you choose?

A] The inauguration of a U.S. president

B] The Opening Ceremonies of an Olympic Games

THINK TWICE!

2 If you had to completely give up one of the following foods for the next five years, which would you find more difficult to forgo?

A] Pizza
B] Hamburgers

THINK TWICE!

3 If you could take a boat tour on either of the following famous rivers, which one would you choose?

A] The Amazon, in South America
B] The Rhine, in Europe

THINK TWICE!

4 From blooming mountain flowers to softly falling leaves ... which of the following seasonal delights would be a more enjoyable experience for you?

A] Springtime in the Rockies
B] Autumn in New England

THINK TWICE!

5 Suppose that, over the course of one month, you had to watch a full year's worth of reruns from either of the following popular comedies of the past. Which would you be spending your evenings watching?

A] *All in the Family*
B] *Leave It To Beaver*

THINK TWICE!

6 You are about to join one of two groups setting out for a month-long summer expedition into the vast and untamed wilderness of northern Canada. You will hike the entire trip, and there will be neither roads nor civilization for one hundred miles in the direction your team will be headed. Each member of the group may fill one small backpack with anything deemed necessary for the trip; however, none of you can know in advance what the others are bringing along. Given this information, and knowing no other details, which of the following two groups would you want to join? (Think very carefully and consider all ramifications ... your life might depend on it!)

A] A group consisting of a biologist, an architect, a gourmet chef, a family counselor, and a former FBI agent.

B] A group consisting of a meteorologist, a professional weightlifter, a nationally respected CEO, a nutritionist, and a journalist

THINK TWICE!

7 If you could travel into the future to see any one thing, which would you be more inclined to choose?

A] Something in the future that specifically involves *you*

B] Something in the future of the country or world at large

THINK TWICE!

8 While walking down a street, you find a black briefcase clearly marked, "Highly confidential information enclosed." Assuming that it isn't locked, what would you be more likely to do?

A] Open it, unable to contain your curiosity

B] Refrain from opening it, turning it in to the police

THINK TWICE!

9 Which of the following not-so-common styles of music would you find more enjoyable?

A] Dixieland
B] Calypso

THINK TWICE!

10 Suppose you owned a very large home with a beautiful circular drive. Which of the following would you be more inclined to place in the center of the circle?

A] The American flag high atop a pole
B] An elegant fountain

THINK TWICE!

If neither you nor anyone else would be hurt, which of the following acts of nature would you find more exciting to witness?

A] A volcano erupting
B] A tidal wave smashing into shore

THINK TWICE!

Which of these annual sports events would you be more interested in sitting down to watch, at least in part?

A] The Kentucky Derby
B] The Indianapolis 500

THINK TWICE!

13 Picture both of the following in your mind for a few seconds. Which scene do you find more peaceful?

A] An old lighthouse on the craggy seashore of Maine

B] A white, high-steepled church in the countryside of Vermont

THINK TWICE!

14 If you were going to be disciplined as an adult, which form of punishment would you find more severe?

A] Having your favorite thing or pastime taken away for thirty days

B] Having to eat something you dislike for one full month

THINK TWICE!

Suppose that you had the power to go back in time and stop either of the following presidential assassinations. You cannot stop both of them; which assassination would you prevent?

A] John F. Kennedy's
B] Abraham Lincoln's

Think Twice!

If you *had* to tell the truth about one of the following in front of a group of people, which would you probably choose to disclose? (If you don't mind telling either, which bit of information do you more freely offer?)

A] Your true age
B] Your true weight

Think Twice!

17 In which of the following high-intensity incidents do you think it would be more exciting to take part?

A] A high-speed freeway chase in a police car

B] A fire department rescue of occupants from a burning high-rise

THINK TWICE!

18 Certainly, words alone cannot describe what these two creative geniuses did, but to have seen or heard their work firsthand . . . If you could travel back in time and witness either of the following men performing their art, which would you choose?

A] Michelangelo painting the Sistine Chapel

B] Bach playing one of his famous concerti on the organ

THINK TWICE!

19 Suppose that you put something into your grocery cart and decided minutes and aisles later that you didn't want it. What would you be more likely to do?

A] Return it to its appropriate location on the shelf

B] Drop it off wherever you happen to be when you decide you don't need it

THINK TWICE!

20 Which of the following romantic activities would you enjoy more?

A] A moonlit walk on the beach

B] A Sunday afternoon picnic for two by the lake

THINK TWICE!

21 Which of these two noncontiguous states is more fascinating to you?

A] Alaska
B] Hawaii

THINK TWICE!

22 Which of these outdoor pests annoys you more?

A] Bees
B] Mosquitoes

THINK TWICE!

23 If you could rid yourself of annoying TV commercials by replacing them with either of the following, which would you choose?

A] Travelogues

B] Trivia questions and answers

THINK TWICE!

24 If you could have either of the following famous homerun balls, which one would you choose?

A] Babe Ruth's 1932 World Series "called shot" homerun ball

B] Hank Aaron's 715th homerun ball that surpassed Ruth for most career homeruns in baseball history

THINK TWICE!

25 If you were sitting on the porch on a warm summer night, which of the following would you find more refreshing?

A] A tall glass of lemonade
B] A large bowl of your favorite ice cream

THINK TWICE!

26 With regard to the goals you set throughout your life, which do you generally find more gratifying?

A] The journey you must take to *reach* that goal
B] The happiness and sense of accomplishment you feel having actually *achieved* the goal

THINK TWICE!

Which of the following outdoor scenes would you find more visually appealing?

A] A large garden of multicolored roses beaded with morning dewdrops

B] A forest of pine trees draped with last night's snow

THINK TWICE!

Which of the following would get your vote for the greater architectural marvel?

A] The Sears Tower in Chicago for its height

B] The Great Wall of China for its length

THINK TWICE!

29 Spots or stripes: which animal do you consider more beautiful?

A] The giraffe
B] The zebra

THINK TWICE!

30 For you, which of the following would be more interesting?

A] To sit on a committee in charge of designing a city of the future
B] To be a part of the greatest archaeological dig of the century

THINK TWICE!

Assuming you can't be all three (healthy, wealthy, *and* wise), which of the following combinations would you want to be?

A] Healthy and wealthy
B] Healthy and wise

THINK TWICE!

Which of the following spectacles do you believe would be more exciting to witness?

A] A daredevil going over Niagara Falls in a barrel
B] A liftoff of the space shuttle

THINK TWICE!

33 In terms of work environment, which of these holds greater appeal for you?

A] An office on the twenty-fifth floor with a window overlooking the city

B] A ground-level office that looks out on trees and a lake

THINK TWICE!

34 If you were put to the test, which of the following do you think you could go longer without?

A] Food

B] Sleep

THINK TWICE!

You've just won an all-expenses-paid trip to either of the following locations. Which one would you choose?

A] A posh hotel in Las Vegas
B] A bed-and-breakfast located in a quaint, historic town

THINK TWICE!

If you were asked to make a Top Ten list of great Americans, which of these famous Toms would you rank closer to the top?

A] Thomas Jefferson
B] Thomas Edison

THINK TWICE!

37 If you could go back in American history to witness either of the following famous battles, which one would you choose?

A] The Battle of the Alamo
B] The Battle of the Little Bighorn (Custer's Last Stand)

THINK TWICE!

38 In your opinion, which of the following watery sounds is more soothing?

A] A gentle rain
B] A rushing stream

THINK TWICE!

39 Suppose that the year is 2100 and technology has allowed for these two futuristic cities to become a reality. In which location would you be more interested in living?

A] An underwater metropolis built on the bottom of one of our oceans

B] A city constructed on another planet's surface

THINK TWICE!

40 For thirty days, you must get away from your usual work routine. Your employer will pay for the leave of absence, but you must choose one of the following for your month-long diversion. Which would you choose?

A] Driving a taxi in New York City

B] Meditating in a secluded monastery or convent

THINK TWICE!

41 While both of the following are usually crowded with people, suppose that for one day you and some friends could have either of them completely to yourselves. Which would you choose?

A] A popular amusement park
B] A professional sports stadium

THINK TWICE!

42 For the sake of personal safety, you may never want to actually attempt either of the following. Nevertheless, which *sounds* more interesting?

A] Rafting the Colorado River in the Grand Canyon
B] Paddling through the waters of the Florida Everglades

THINK TWICE!

43 Even as an adult, which of these childlike activities would be more fun for you?

A] Building a tree house
B] Creating a large castle in a giant sandbox

T H I N K   T W I C E !

44 While attending a party at a friend's house, you happen to notice the following two personal items of the host/hostess lying on the kitchen table. Nobody is around; which would you be more tempted to peek at?

A] Their wallet
B] Their checkbook

T H I N K   T W I C E !

45 On which of these cruises would you be more interested in embarking?

A] An Alaskan cruise
B] A Caribbean cruise

THINK TWICE!

46 You are about to leave on a long road trip. There's one condition: you may take only one CD or cassette tape with you, and you must choose from the two listed below. Which will it be? (Assume that using the radio is not an option.)

A] *Gershwin's Greatest Works*
B] *The King's Greatest Rock 'n' Roll Hits*

THINK TWICE!

47 If your community wished to honor you for something great that you had done, which of the following would you rather have named after you?

A] A street
B] A building

THINK TWICE!

48 If both of the following popular fictional characters were running for office, which would get your vote?

A] Snoopy
B] Mickey Mouse

THINK TWICE!

49 If you had to describe your personality in terms of one of the following vehicles, which would come closer to "the real you"?

A] A pickup truck
B] A convertible

THINK TWICE!

50 Some of the most memorable quotes have come from U.S. presidents. For whatever your reason, which of these famous inaugural quotations do you feel is more powerful?

A] "Ask not what your country can do for you; ask what you can do for your country."
    —John F. Kennedy
B] "The only thing we have to fear is fear itself."
    —Franklin D. Roosevelt

THINK TWICE!

51 When situations or opportunities involving risk present themselves, which is your more likely response?

A] Play it safe

B] Take your chances

THINK TWICE!

52 If you could be temporarily miniaturized to the size of a human cell or grain of sand (and would be safe in either case), which of the following do you think would be more fun to explore?

A] The inside of the human body

B] The insect world within a cubic foot of soil

THINK TWICE!

53 Suppose that you were given the professional ability to achieve either of the following one time without injuring yourself. Which do you think would be more fun to experience?

A] Riding a bull for eight seconds in the rodeo
B] Completing a jump in the Olympic ski-jump competition

THINK TWICE!

54 In your opinion, which of the following would the average person find more amusing?

A] The way you laugh
B] The way you sneeze

THINK TWICE!

Forget fat grams! In which of the following classic combinations would you rather indulge yourself?

A] Coffee and doughnuts
B] Cookies and milk

THINK TWICE!

In peacetime, for fun, which of the following would you rather do?

A] Go down in a nuclear submarine
B] Go up in a fighter jet

THINK TWICE!

57 When socializing at a party or in any other group of people, which do you generally prefer to do more?

A] Talk
B] Listen

THINK TWICE!

58 Which of the following famous New York City streets do you believe gives the city more of its identity?

A] Broadway
B] Wall Street

THINK TWICE!

59 In your opinion, which of the following would be a more ideal location for a vacation home?

A] Up in the mountains, looking down on a beautiful valley

B] Down in a valley or basin, surrounded by breathtaking mountains

THINK TWICE!

60 Which of the following would be a more relaxing way for you to unwind?

A] A fifteen-minute massage

B] Thirty minutes in a Jacuzzi

THINK TWICE!

61 Which of these high-flying experiences would you enjoy more?

A] A hot-air balloon ride over the countryside
B] Hang gliding over a lake

THINK TWICE!

62 If you were given the opportunity to have a one-on-one dinner with either of the following high-profile people, whom would you choose?

A] The pope
B] The president

THINK TWICE!

63 If you were in excellent health and found yourself at a playground, which would you be more inclined to get on?

A] A swing
B] A merry-go-round

THINK TWICE!

64 Which of the following European "adventures" would you find more intriguing?

A] A tour of England's castles
B] A tour of Norway's fjords

THINK TWICE!

65 Movies, books, and magazines have long romanticized the following pieces of American history, still existing today. Which do you consider more romantic?

A] Covered bridges
B] Southern antebellum mansions

THINK TWICE!

66 Which weather scenario would you receive more favorably?

A] The warmth of an early spring following a frigid winter
B] The chill of an early autumn following a blistering summer

THINK TWICE!

You're walking with a friend at the mall when you spot a $50 bill lying on the ground about fifteen feet in front of the two of you. You don't know if your friend would have spotted it if *your* eyes hadn't seen it so quickly. What would you do?

A] Finders, keepers—keep the money for yourself
B] Split the money with your friend

THINK TWICE!

Most of us would love to be famous for one thing or another. Which of the following claims to fame would you rather have?

A] A *New York Times* bestselling author
B] An Academy award–winning actor/actress

THINK TWICE!

69 If you could go back in time and take an in-depth behind-the-scenes look at either of the following political crises, which would you choose?

A] The Cuban missile crisis
B] Watergate

THINK TWICE!

70 Some of the most famous people ever in their respective fields have been gathered together for an awards dinner. Two of the tables have an empty seat, and you're the lucky guest who has been invited to fill one of them. Exactly who you will sit *next to* at the table is unknown, so you must choose based on the table as a whole. Think carefully: with which group would you want to be seated for dinner? (Assume that everyone would speak English.)

A] Mozart, Mark Twain, Leonardo da Vinci, Napoléon Bonaparte, and Amelia Earhart
B] Walt Disney, William Shakespeare, Socrates, Albert Einstein, and Joan of Arc

THINK TWICE!

71   If you could look into the future of the world,
how far down the road would you like to see?

A] Twenty-five years from now
B] Two hundred fifty years from now

THINK TWICE!

72   If a bowl of each of the following were placed
in front of you, which would you reach for
first?

A] Popcorn
B] Potato chips

THINK TWICE!

73 A national newspaper has informed you that, upon your death, it is going to write an article in memory of your life. In this case, however, the paper has asked you to choose the *angle* of the story in advance of your passing. Which of these would you tell the newspaper to focus on?

A] An admirable act or accomplishment in your life
B] A principle by which you lived your life

THINK TWICE!

74 Which of these businesses would you be more inclined to open if you had both the money and the opportunity?

A] Your own restaurant
B] Your own retail store

THINK TWICE!

Suppose you were offered $5,000 to read, over a six-month period, one of the following from cover to cover. Which would you be more likely to choose?

A] Webster's Dictionary
B] The Holy Bible

Think Twice!

Suppose you sat down in front of a coffee table on which were laid the following two items. Which would you be more likely to pick up?

A] The current issue of *Time* magazine
B] A photography book featuring U.S. city skylines

Think Twice!

77 Most people would agree that fountains are lovely—to both see *and* hear. Which aspect of a fountain do you consider more beautiful?

A] The sight of the water
B] The sound of the water

THINK TWICE!

78 Which of the following well-known quotes from the American Revolution gets your vote for being more emotionally patriotic?

A] "I know not what course others may take, but as for me, give me liberty or give me death!"
                    —Patrick Henry, 1775
B] "I only regret that I have but one life to lose for my country."
                    —Nathan Hale, 1776

THINK TWICE!

If a movie producer decided to do a movie about your life, under which category would the film more than likely fall?

A] Comedy
B] Drama

THINK TWICE!

In which of the following situations would you feel more psychologically uncomfortable?

A] A thirty-second elevator ride—just you and a stranger of the opposite sex all the way up
B] A sixty-minute plane ride—you sitting next to a stranger of the same sex on a crowded flight

THINK TWICE!

45

81 In your opinion, which of the following better symbolizes the word *happiness*?

A] A butterfly
B] A rainbow

THINK TWICE!

82 Let go of any inhibitions for a moment. Which of these seasonal activities would be more fun for you?

A] Raking a huge pile of leaves and jumping into it
B] Building a snowman after a heavy snowfall

THINK TWICE!

83 Which of the following trips would you be more enthusiastic about taking?

A] A tour of America's most beautiful national parks
B] A tour of America's most famous historic places

THINK TWICE!

84 If you could experience either of the following, which would you choose?

A] A five-minute one-on-one game against a professional basketball player
B] Ten pitches in which to get a base hit against a professional baseball pitcher

THINK TWICE!

85 If you could listen to only one type of music for one full year and had to make your musical choice from the two types listed below, which would you choose?

A] Patriotic music
B] Christmas music

THINK TWICE!

86 Which of the following out-of-the-ordinary vacations would you be more interested in taking? (Assume all expenses are covered.)

A] An African safari
B] A tour of the Holy Land

THINK TWICE!

87 For a few seconds, forget about temperature preferences and think with your nose. Which season's scents do you enjoy more?

A] Spring
B] Fall

THINK TWICE!

88 If you could step back into the 1800s and safely witness either of the following, which one would you choose?

A] A gun duel in a western town
B] A buffalo stampede on the prairie

THINK TWICE!

89 Not your typical day at the beach. Which one of these activities sounds like more fun?

A]   Whale watching off the coast
B]   Snorkeling in a coral reef

THINK TWICE!

90 If you could have either of the following to make your life easier and/or less stressful, which one would you choose?

A]   A personal housekeeper
B]   A personal chauffeur

THINK TWICE!

91 If your house were on fire and you had time to save only one item, which would you be more likely to choose? (Assume all people and pets are safely outside.)

A] Something of great monetary value
B] Something of great sentimental value

THINK TWICE!

92 Which of the following do you consider to be the greater American icon?

A] Mount Rushmore
B] The Golden Gate Bridge

THINK TWICE!

93 If, for one month, you had the opportunity to work with professionals in training either of the following animals, which would you choose?

A] Elephants
B] Dolphins

THINK TWICE!

94 Which of the following daily activities do you perform more meticulously?

A] Brushing/flossing your teeth
B] Brushing/combing your hair

THINK TWICE!

Which of these are you more likely to put off until the last minute?

A] Filing your income tax return
B] Buying Christmas gifts

THINK TWICE!

Being inundated by advertisers can certainly be annoying; but if you could be on the other side, working in the field, which type of advertising would you prefer to create?

A] Beautiful print ads for popular magazines
B] Entertaining commercials for national television

THINK TWICE!

97 If you were given two twenty-five-question trivia tests from the following categories, on which subject would you expect to fare better?

A] World history
B] World geography

THINK TWICE!

98 You know what they say: plan today for tomorrow. Which of the following do you think would be more exciting to create?

A] A futuristic mode of transportation
B] A futuristic recreational/sports activity

THINK TWICE!

99 If you had the chance to work for the president of the United States in either of the following capacities, which would you choose?

A] Speechwriter
B] Secret Service

THINK TWICE!

100 Which of the following accents do you find more charming?

A] The accent of someone from the Deep South
B] The accent of someone from England

THINK TWICE!

101 Which of the following TV talk-show interviews would you be more interested in watching?

A] A discussion with a famous political figure
B] A one-on-one conversation with a movie star

THINK TWICE!

102 Which of the following settings would you find more conducive to inner reflection and meditation?

A] A beautiful cathedral with stained-glass windows
B] A serene lake at sunset

THINK TWICE!

103 There are two surprise gifts under the Christmas tree. One box is 4″ square; the other box is 18″ square. Assuming that no shaking is allowed and you can have only one, which gift would you choose?

A] The 4″ square box
B] The 18″ square box

THINK TWICE!

104 Which of these famous journeys/discoveries do you think would've been more exciting?

A] Columbus's voyage and "discovery" of the New World
B] Lewis and Clark's expedition of the unknown land west of the Mississippi

THINK TWICE!

105 Which of the following annual events do you generally find more exciting and/or exhilirating?

A] The grand finale of the fireworks display on Independence Day

B] The 60-second countdown to midnight on New Year's Eve

THINK TWICE!

106 Which of the following would be more difficult for you to give up completely?

A] Coffee

B] Chocolate

THINK TWICE!

107 We often take much of what we have for granted, forgetting that there was a time when modern-day conveniences were unimaginable. Without which of these inventions is it harder to imagine life?

A] The telephone
B] The electric light

THINK TWICE!

108 If you could possess either of the following special abilities, which would you prefer?

A] The power to read someone's mind
B] The power to make yourself invisible

THINK TWICE!

109 A popular bumper sticker reads, "He who dies with the most toys wins." The following are two nonmaterialistic alternatives; which one do you like better?

A] "He who dies with the most friends wins"
B] "He who dies with the most wisdom wins"

THINK TWICE!

110 If you had the chance to see your favorite athlete in either of the following situations, which one would you choose?

A] Dinner with the athlete at an elegant restaurant
B] A front-row seat to see the sports star play in a championship game

THINK TWICE!

111 If it were somehow possible for you to join either of the following fictional characters in their adventures and experiences, whom would you choose?

A] Huckleberry Finn
B] Robinson Crusoe

THINK TWICE!

112 Which of the following, if a very stirring rendition were performed, would be more likely to bring a patriotic lump to your throat?

A] *The Star-Spangled Banner*
B] *The Battle Hymn of the Republic*

THINK TWICE!

113 Some first-time visitors to the United States want to see both of the following during their stay, but only have time to visit one or the other. Which would you recommend?

A] Yellowstone National Park
B] Walt Disney World

THINK TWICE!

114 Suppose that, for fun, you could acquire either of the following animal characteristics for one day. Which would you choose?

A] The powerful jumping ability of a kangaroo
B] The skillful tree-climbing ability of a monkey

THINK TWICE!

115 Which of these household chores do you dislike more?

A] Dusting
B] Ironing

116 If you had the opportunity to witness either of the following scenes being filmed for a Hollywood movie, which one would you choose?

A] A gasoline truck exploding
B] An automobile being struck by a fast-moving train

117 Suppose that an American who died in the year 1800 was brought back for a brief period in order to catch a glimpse of how our country has changed since then. Which of the following do you think our guest would find harder to believe?

A] The technological advances
B] The sociological changes

THINK TWICE!

118 You are hiking a wilderness trail when suddenly you come to a fork in the path. One way leads *up* and runs along the top of the cliffs; the other leads *down* and runs along the river. Which path would you travel?

A] The trail along the river
B] The trail atop the cliffs

THINK TWICE!

119 Which of the following do you consider more offensive?

A] The sound of nails scraping a chalkboard
B] The smell of skunk fumes

THINK TWICE!

120 If you could choose only one, which of the following would you like to hear more often from more people?

A] "Thank you; I appreciate what you've done."
B] "I'm sorry; I was wrong."

THINK TWICE!

121 Each of the following is truly a wonder of nature. In your opinion, which is more amazing?

A] The giant sequoia trees of California
B] The geysers and hot springs of Yellowstone

THINK TWICE!

122 In everyday conversation, which of these typical topics are you *less* interested in hearing about from someone else?

A] Their family
B] Their job

THINK TWICE!

123 If you could take a pill that would protect you from ever again suffering either of the following, which would you choose?

A] Headaches

B] Stomach aches

124 Suppose that both of the following were completely removed from your life for one full year. Which loss would be harder for you to take?

A] Television/VCR

B] Music (radio, CDs, tapes)

THINK TWICE!

125 If someone offered you the following monetary choice, which would you accept?

A] $2,500 cash in your hand today
B] $5,000 in a savings account that can't be withdrawn for two full years

THINK TWICE!

126 For which of these products would you be a more enthusiastic spokesperson?

A] Your favorite food
B] Your favorite beverage

THINK TWICE!

127 If you could spend a two-week vacation on either of these continents, which one would you choose?

A] Africa
B] Australia

THINK TWICE!

128 Suppose that whenever you became extremely frustrated or angry, you could enter a special room with a brick wall and have either of the following at your disposal to hurl against it. Which would you choose?

A] A bushel basket of ripe tomatoes
B] A crate of empty glass bottles

THINK TWICE!

129 Suppose that the daily weather scenario never changed—never! Which of the following would you rather see as a permanent forecast?

A] Eighty degrees and mostly cloudy
B] Forty degrees and mostly sunny

THINK TWICE!

130 From which of the following famous historic documents could you recite more from memory?

A] The Bill of Rights
B] The Gettysburg Address

THINK TWICE!

131 Which of these do you think would be more fun to explore?

A] A sunken pirate ship
B] The ruins of an ancient Indian temple

THINK TWICE!

132 Suppose that you would actually feel better and be far more efficient with one hour less sleep than you currently get. If this were true, which would you be more likely to do?

A] Wake up an hour earlier
B] Stay up an hour later

THINK TWICE!

133 Which of the following sensory experiences would your feet enjoy more?

A] Walking on warm sand on a beach
B] Walking through cool, green grass

THINK TWICE!

134 The sound. The sensation. The excitement. If you could safely experience either of the following, which would you choose?

A] Standing at the end of a runway at a major airport
B] Standing on the edge of a racetrack during a professional auto race

THINK TWICE!

135 Which of the following would make you queasier quicker?

A] The sight of blood
B] The sight of an injection with a needle

THINK TWICE!

136 If you were in Washington, D.C., for one day and had only a few hours to do "the tourist thing," which of the following would you be more inclined to do?

A] Visit Arlington National Cemetery
B] Tour the Smithsonian

THINK TWICE!

137 As an adult, which of these annual activities would you enjoy doing more?

A] Coloring Easter eggs
B] Carving a Halloween pumpkin

THINK TWICE!

138 Assuming that your home team was not playing in either one, which of the following sports events would you enjoy watching more?

A] The Super Bowl
B] The seventh game of the NBA Finals

THINK TWICE!

139 Which do you feel you know more about?

A] Your family's history
B] American history

THINK TWICE!

140 Which of the following creates a more beautiful picture in your mind's eye?

A] Streams, lakes, and waterfalls
B] Fields, flowers, and trees

THINK TWICE!

141 Suppose that you had the power to save one of the following from destruction, but had to accept the leveling of the other. Which would you save?

A] The Lincoln Memorial
B] The Statue of Liberty

THINK TWICE!

142 In which of the following ways do you prefer the toilet tissue to unfurl in your bathroom?

A] From underneath the roll
B] From over the top of the roll

THINK TWICE!

143 Forty-two of one, fifty of the other. From which of the following categories do you think you could recite a greater percentage of the total?

A] U.S. presidents
B] U.S. state capitals

THINK TWICE!

144 If it were loose in your house, which of the following would frighten you more?

A] A small bat
B] A large snake

THINK TWICE!

145 Which of the following annually televised events would you be more likely to take time to watch, at least in part?

A] The president's State of the Union address

B] The New Year's Day Tournament of Roses Parade

THINK TWICE!

146 If you were on a train ride in the mountains, which of the following would be a greater highlight of the trip for you?

A] Going over a long, high bridge

B] Going through a long, dark tunnel

THINK TWICE!

147 For one full week, you will be provided with the following three things at absolutely no expense: a private jet, a personal pilot, and unlimited fuel. Which would you be more inclined to do?

A] Fly somewhere you've always wanted to visit, enjoy a relaxing stay, and fly back at week's end

B] Fly to as many locations as you can possibly cram into a seven-day period

148 What's in a name? You're the first to arrive at a party when you see the following two name tags lying on a table. Judging strictly by the name, with whom do you think you would enjoy conversing more?

A] William Robert Smith III

B] Billy Bob Smith

149 If you could have one trip in a time machine, which direction would you be more likely to go?

A] Back to the past
B] Forward into the future

THINK TWICE!

150 If you could instantly become one of America's leading experts in either of the following fields, which one would you choose?

A] Law
B] Medicine

THINK TWICE!

151 In both of these job situations, you would receive the exact same salary, and a decent one at that. Which would you rather work?

A] Thirty hours a week at a job where you're generally unhappy

B] Sixty hours a week at a job that you generally enjoy

THINK TWICE!

152 When you think of American history, which of these two presidents is foremost in your mind?

A] George Washington

B] Abraham Lincoln

THINK TWICE!

153 If you could go back in time to witness either of the following major achievements in our history, which would you choose?

A] Building the Panama Canal

B] Laying the transcontinental railroad that connected the west to the rest

THINK TWICE!

154 If you could have either of the following, which would you choose?

A] Guaranteed perfect health and safety for the next five years

B] $50,000 in cash today

THINK TWICE!

155 A movie critic on TV is about to discuss a hot new movie that you definitely intend to see. You know that there is supposed to be an incredible surprise ending—an ending the critic will surely discuss—but you have not as yet heard what the ending is. What would you do?

A] Change the channel so the surprise is not ruined for you

B] Listen to the surprise ending so that you know what to expect

THINK TWICE!

156 For fifteen minutes, you are placed in a room with nothing more than a table, a chair, and two small items on top of the table. Which item would you be more likely to play with to help pass the time?

A] The paper clip

B] The penny

THINK TWICE!

157 Your team is down by one, there are three seconds on the clock, and the basketball is in your hands. You and three other teammates are being closely guarded; you could pass to your fifth teammate who is wide open for a final shot, but he/she is not quite as good a shooter as you. What do you do?

A] Pass the ball to the open teammate

B] Under close guard, put the final shot in the air yourself

THINK TWICE!

158 Forget the calculator and spell checker. Which of the following refresher courses would do you more good?

A] Spelling 101

B] Math 101

THINK TWICE!

159 If you had the chance to celebrate Christmas in either of the following locations, which one would you choose?

A] The snowy mountains of Vermont
B] Colonial Williamsburg

THINK TWICE!

160 If you were offered ownership of either of the following, which one would you choose?

A] A professional sports team
B] A small tropical island ripe for tourism

THINK TWICE!

161 If you could experience either of the following out-of-the-ordinary summer vacations with a group of people, which would you choose?

A] Spending a week on a dude ranch
B] Hiking the Appalachian Trail for a week

THINK TWICE!

162 If you could have either of the following special powers that you could effectively use at will, which would you choose?

A] The power to change someone's opinion
B] The power to change someone's personality

THINK TWICE!

163 Suppose that tomorrow someone came to your door, announcing that you had won a contest and presenting you with a check for $200,000. Now, be honest: What percent of your instant winnings would you be willing to give away to others, expecting nothing in return?

A] 20 percent or more
B] Less than 20 percent

THINK TWICE!

164 Curiosity may have killed the cat, but we humans seem to thrive on it. If you had the opportunity to do either of the following, which would you choose?

A] Sneak a peek at a close friend's personal diary
B] Learn the secret to a mind-boggling, unbelievable magic trick

THINK TWICE!

165 Suppose that a mandatory job transfer offered you either of the following two cities for relocation. Which would you choose?

A] Bangor, Maine
B] Santa Fe, New Mexico

THINK TWICE!

166 When conversing with friends or acquaintances, which of the following do you do more often?

A] Praise a product, place, or service with which you are very happy
B] Discredit a product, place, or service with which you are very displeased

THINK TWICE!

167 If you could have dinner and spend the evening in either of the following famous residences, which would you choose? (Assume that in neither case would the president nor the royalty be present.)

A] The White House
B] Buckingham Palace

THINK TWICE!

168 Which of the following events do you believe will happen first? *Think very carefully!*

A] The Chicago Cubs win the World Series
B] The "Big One" hits California

THINK TWICE!

169 If you had the chance to experience either of the following events, which would you choose?

A] A small-town, old-fashioned Fourth of July celebration
B] Mardi Gras in New Orleans

THINK TWICE!

170 With regard to famous people of the past, (composers, presidents, explorers, etc.), which of the following trivial bits of information generally interests you more?

A] Their date of birth
B] Their date of death

THINK TWICE!

171 You should be able to answer this question in a snap—or a whistle! Which of the following is easier for you to do?

A] Snap your fingers loudly

B] Whistle a tune

THINK TWICE!

172 If you had the opportunity to achieve either of the following, which would you find more exciting?

A] Winning a national championship as a key player for a professional sports team

B] Winning an individual gold medal in the Olympic Games

THINK TWICE!

173 Which of the following would be more frightening for you?

A] Delivering a thirty-minute speech to an audience of a thousand people

B] Spending one night alone in an old house that is supposedly haunted

THINK TWICE!

174 If you had to choose one of the following great quotes as your epitaph, which would you choose?

A] "A life is not important except in the impact it has on other lives."
　　　　　—Jackie Robinson

B] "Nothing is small which serves a larger purpose."
　　　　　—Horace Mann

THINK TWICE!

175 If you could be instantly endowed with either of the following, which would you choose?

A] Incredible speed
B] Incredible strength

THINK TWICE!

176 If you could go back in time to witness either of the following, which would you prefer to see?

A] A famous moment in sports history
B] A famous moment in political history

THINK TWICE!

177 Jack-of-all-trades or master of one? Which of the following would you rather be?

A] Exceptionally gifted at one thing, but fairly poor at most everything else

B] Fairly good at most things, but not exceptional at anything

THINK TWICE!

178 If you had one hour to carefully study either of the following, to which would you direct your concentration?

A] A globe of the world

B] An atlas of the United States

THINK TWICE!

179 In your opinion, which of the following animals is cuter?

A] A panda bear
B] A koala bear

THINK TWICE!

180 Which of the following big-city jobs—more than the other—could they not pay you enough to perform?

A] Inspecting the city sewers
B] Cleaning the outside windows on tall buildings

THINK TWICE!

181 If you could lie down in an open field in the country and enjoy either of the following, which would you be more likely to do?

A] Watch cloud formations roll by on a lazy summer afternoon

B] Watch the stars twinkle on a clear summer night

THINK TWICE!

182 If, as the winner of a supermarket contest, you could receive fifty free jars of either of the following, which would you choose?

A] Salsa

B] Peanut butter

THINK TWICE!

183 If you could spend a week's vacation in either of the following European countries, which location would you grace with your presence?

A] France
B] Italy

THINK TWICE!

184 If you had to rank one of the following battles as being greater than the other, which would come out on top? (Define *greater* however you wish.)

A] Gettysburg
B] Normandy Beach

THINK TWICE!

185 It seems like there is never enough time to do it all, and yet by the time the big day arrives, many of us are completely wiped out. If you could do either of the following to the Christmas season, which would it be?

A] Make it longer
B] Make it shorter

THINK TWICE!

186 When watching your favorite professional team play a rival team, what type of scenario do you generally prefer?

A] A good, close game that goes right down to the very end
B] A blowout game where your team routs the opposition

THINK TWICE!

187 Which of the following late superstars would you rank higher on a list of the top ten TV celebrities of all time?

A] Jackie Gleason
B] Lucille Ball

THINK TWICE!

188 Which of the following "games" would you be more inclined to try if both were lying in front of you?

A] A crossword puzzle
B] A jigsaw puzzle

THINK TWICE!

189 Assuming that each of the following is extremely high-powered, which would you have more fun using on a day-to-day (or night-to-night) basis?

A] A microscope
B] A telescope

THINK TWICE!

190 If you could spend a full day at either of the following public places, which one would you probably enjoy more?

A] A top-ranked museum
B] An acclaimed zoological park

THINK TWICE!

191 If by taking a pill you could instantly be either of the following, which would you want to be?

A] Taller than you are
B] Smarter than you are

THINK TWICE!

192 In which of the following situations do you generally find yourself having less patience?

A] Sitting in traffic
B] Standing in line

THINK TWICE!

193 Throughout Olympic history (or as much as you can remember), which of the following do you believe has provided more memorable moments for the world?

A] The Summer Games
B] The Winter Games

THINK TWICE!

194 Which direction do you generally lick an ice-cream cone?

A] From left to right
B] From right to left

THINK TWICE!

195 If you could be either of the following highly publicized celebrity types, which would you want to be?

A] A chart-topping musical performer
B] A popular TV talk-show host

THINK TWICE!

196 If you had the opportunity to help field researchers study either of the following ecosystems, which would you find more fascinating?

A] The Sahara Desert
B] A South American rain forest

THINK TWICE!

197 Pretend that videotape doesn't exist. If you could leave behind only one of the following for family and friends to remember you by, which would you choose?

A] A photo album with pictures of you throughout your life

B] A cassette recording of you talking about your favorite memories

THINK TWICE!

198 If a professional offered to do either of the following for you at no expense, which one would you want?

A] A portrait of yourself

B] A statue of your likeness

THINK TWICE!

199 If you could travel back in time to serve as a reporter for one week, observing the excitement in either of the following famous cities, which one would you choose?

A] Philadelphia, Pennsylvania, 1787
B] San Francisco, California, 1849

THINK TWICE!

200 If you could "be there" to witness either of the following fantastic finishes in sports, which one would you choose?

A] A professional golfer sinking a sixty-foot putt on the eighteenth hole to win the U.S. Open
B] A home team World Series-winning homerun in the bottom of the ninth.

THINK TWICE!

201 Picture yourself curled up in your favorite chair with your favorite book or magazine. Now, which of the following sounds would you find more relaxing?

A] The rhythmic ticking of a grandfather clock

B] The erratic crackling of wood in a fireplace

THINK TWICE!

202 You are offered $100 if you can accurately identify the object in either of two boxes, each of which contains a different item. One item can be identified by the smell; the other by the touch. While neither object can hurt you, you have been told that both are considered unpleasant to most people. The blindfold is on; which would you be more willing to try and guess?

A] The thing that requires your sense of smell

B] The thing that requires your sense of touch

THINK TWICE!

203 You are being dropped off by boat on a remote, tropical island that modern civilization knows nothing about. You will spend four weeks there, without companions, and it is your job to, quite simply, stay alive. As you disembark the craft, you are told that you may take absolutely nothing with you except the clothes you are wearing and one of the following. Which would you choose?

A] A shotgun with six cartridges

B] A first-aid kit complete with large bandages, medicines, and antidotes

THINK TWICE!

204 Suppose that every day, as far as the weather goes, had to be split down the middle: one half with beautiful sunshine and the other half filled with clouds of gray. Assuming that the order had to be the same every day, how would you want your days divided?

A] Dismal, cloudy mornings with bright, sunny afternoons

B] Bright, sunny mornings with dismal, overcast afternoons

THINK TWICE!

205 Which of the following do you believe would be a more frightening situation? (Assume that in both cases the beast is only 50 yards in front of you.)

A] Encountering a Great White shark while swimming in the ocean

B] Encountering an African lion while walking through the woods

THINK TWICE!

206 The two events listed below are often considered to be among the most important in history. Which would you say has had a greater impact on the world as we know it? *Think very carefully!*

A] Johann Gutenberg's mass-production of the written word . . . and the subsequent information epidemic

B] Thomas Jefferson's penning of the Declaration of Independence . . . and the democratic ideals contained therein

THINK TWICE!

About the Authors

Bret Nicholaus and **Paul Lowrie** are 1991 graduates of Bethel College, St. Paul, Minnesota. They hold their degrees in public relations/advertising and marketing, respectively. Nicholaus lives in the Chicago, IL, area; Lowrie is a resident of South Dakota. Both authors are product developers, firmly committed to providing positive entertainment for adults and children alike. They have collaborated on three previous popular books, *The Conversation Piece*, *The Christmas Conversation Piece*, and *The Mom & Dad Conversation Piece*. Bret and Paul are the creators of the nationally syndicated radio program *The Conversation Piece*, based on their question book of the same title.

Both authors would love to hear how you are using *Think Twice!* or any of their previous books. You may write to them at the address below:

Brett Nicholaus & Paul Lowrie
P.O. Box 340, Yankton, SD 57078